Contents

D1710096

Unit 1: Ideas

Unit 2: Organization

Unit 3: Word Choice

 **Ideas** A good topic is clear.

A. Choose the best topic. Underline the topic that gives a clear idea of each picture.

animal homes
animals that live in trees

a dog with a special job
a nice dog

ocean animals
ocean animals with shells

Tabby and her kittens
pet cats

B. Choose a zoo animal. Write a clear topic about it.

Animal: _The tiger._

Topic: _The tiger has fur._

 **Ideas** A good topic is interesting.

A. Read the stories. Then write the topic of each one.

My name is cha-cha. I am mason's pet dog. I am smart and cute. I meet him at the door. Then I do a dance!

Topic:

_____

My name is star. I am a pony. claire and I ride in horse shows. We win ribbons.

Topic:

_____

I am a bunny. I like to chase dogs. I run around the house. My name is puff.

Topic:

_____

B. Reread the stories. Fix the words that should be capitalized.

  Daily 6-Trait Writing • EMC 6792 • © Evan-Moor Corp.

 **Ideas** Choose a specific topic.

Read each topic. Write two ways to make the topic more interesting. Circle the one you like best.

Topic: fun at school

1. _____

2. _____

Topic: uncommon pets

1. _____

2. _____

Topic: eating dinner

1. _____

2. _____

Topic: bears

1. _____

2. _____

 **Ideas** Choose a narrow topic.

Complete the triangle. Narrow your ideas.

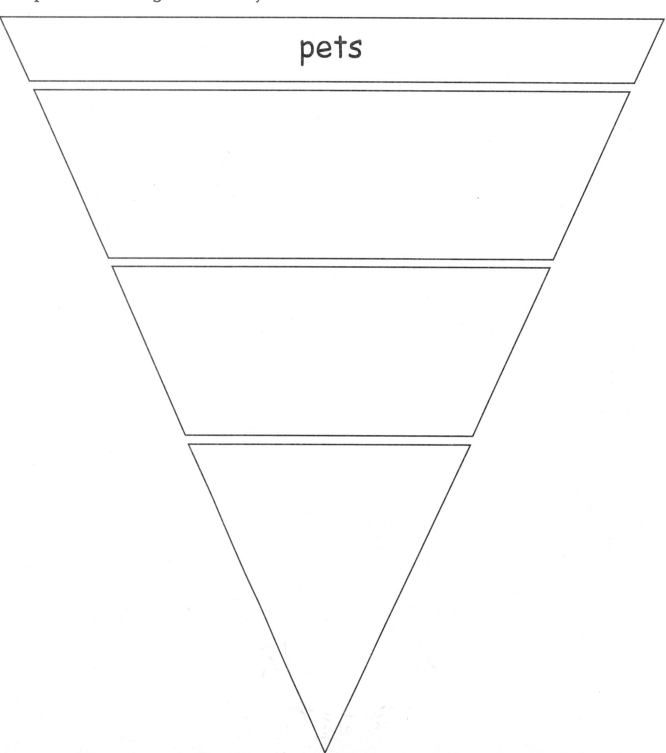

pets

 **Ideas**

Write about a pet. Use the topic you chose on Day 4.
Be sure to capitalize the names of people and pets.

_____

_____

_____

_____

_____

_____

_____

_____

_____

_____

_____

Pet

 **Ideas** Details tell more about the topic.

A. Read this thank-you note. Underline the details that tell about the topic. Then circle the four compound words in Carlos's note.

> Dear Aunt Suzi,
>
> Thank you for taking me birthday shopping! I like my new brown raincoat. It matches my brown boots. I can wear it zipped up. The hood will keep me warm. The best thing is the soft, furry inside.
>
> Thank you for making my birthday special! May I go shopping with you again next year?
>
> Love,
>
> Carlos

B. Draw a picture of Carlos in his new raincoat. Label the picture with the details Carlos wrote.

 **Ideas** Add details to tell more about the topic.

A. Read this story. Then list four details you read.

A Shoe Is Born

I was born in a poor old shoemaker's shop. He cut me out of his very last piece of leather. Then he placed me on his workbench. He went home. Late that night, two tiny elves danced into the shop. The elves worked and worked until sunrise. Then they ran off. The next morning, the shoemaker had a big surprise. I was a pair of beautiful red shoes!

1. _____

2. _____

3. _____

4. _____

B. Write the four different compound words in the story.

_____   _____

_____   _____

Ideas Add details to make your writing more interesting.

A. Read about what Kayla likes to wear. Draw a line under each detail.

My Racing T-Shirt
by Kayla

Do you know what I like to wear best? It's my white T-shirt. I got it last year at the racetrack. It has a picture of car number seven. The car is bright green. I hope to get a new shirt this year at the race!

B. Read Tina's paragraph. She needs to add more details. Look at the picture and write three details she missed.

My New T-Shirt
by Tina

My new T-shirt is my favorite thing to wear. I saw it at the store. My grandmother bought it for me. It is pretty.

Details:

1. _____

2. _____

3. _____

C. Find the two compound words in the stories. Draw a line between the two smaller words.

 **Ideas** Add details to make your writing more interesting.

Imagine your shoe could tell you about its life. Fill in the topic.
Write a detail for each question.

Topic: The Life of _____

Details:

What does it
look like?   _____

                  _____

What does
it do?   _____

                  _____

Where does
it go?   _____

                  _____

What does
it like?   _____

                  _____

What doesn't
it like?   _____

                  _____

 **Ideas**

Imagine your shoe could tell you about its life. Write what it would say. Use the details you listed on Day 4.

Try to use at least one compound word in your writing.

_____

_____

_____

_____

_____

_____

_____

_____

_____

_____

_____

_____

_____

_____

Daily 6-Trait Writing • EMC 6792 • © Evan-Moor Corp.

 **Ideas** Good details give important, interesting information.

A. Read the two paragraphs. Draw a line under each interesting detail. Mark an **X** in the box by the paragraph that has better details.

Milk from Cows

☐ Did you know that milk comes from cows? Cows live on a farm. A farmer feeds the cows. The cows like different kinds of food. Mother cows make milk. The farmer milks the cows. Then he sends the milk to a factory. From there it goes to the store where you can buy it.

Get Milk!

☐ The milk you drink comes from cows. Cows live on a dairy farm. A dairy farmer feeds the cows. Did you know that cows eat cereal like you do? Sometimes they even eat cookies or potato chips. They like hay, corn, and grass, too. A mother cow's body makes milk. The farmer milks the cows. He sends the milk to a factory. The factory puts the milk into cartons. Then the cartons go by truck to the store.

B. Change the sentence. Add an interesting detail.

A farmer feeds his cows.

_____

_____

C. Circle the plural nouns that end in s in both paragraphs.

 **Ideas** Choose details that are important and interesting.

A. Read the description. Draw a line under the details that tell how a tomato grows.

Tomato Garden

Would you like to grow tomatoes? They are grown from tomato seeds. Plant the seeds in a sunny place. Give them water every day. The plants will grow tall. Soon, they will be thick with leaves. One day, small yellow flowers will peek out of the leaves. Days later, a green tomato will grow under each flower! The tomatoes will grow bigger. They will turn yellow and then red-orange. When the tomatoes are big and red, pick one. It will be the best one you ever tasted!

B. Think about a tomato. What does the skin look and feel like? What does the inside look and feel like? Write an interesting detail sentence about a tomato.

_____

_____

C. Make these nouns plural. Add an **s**.

seed_____   plant_____   flower_____   day_____

 **Ideas** Choose details that are important and interesting.

A. Read the paragraph. Then write a sentence with an interesting detail to add to the end of the story.

From the Field to Your Lunch

Do you have a slice of bread in your lunch today? It came from a farmer's field! Here's how it happened. A farmer plowed up his field. Next, he planted wheat seeds. He watered the wheat. He got rid of bugs and weeds. When the wheat was ripe, the farmer picked it. If bad weather came, it could hurt the wheat. So he worked for days to pick it. Then, he sold the wheat. It was ground into flour, and the flour was baked into bread.

Ending Sentence:

_____

_____

_____

B. Write four nouns from the story that name more than one person, place, or thing.

_____   _____

_____   _____

 **Ideas** Choose details that are important and interesting.

Tell about your favorite bread. Write interesting details.

Topic:

My favorite bread: _____

Details:

What I eat on it: _____

When I eat it: _____

Where I eat it: _____

Whom I eat it with: _____

Why I like it: _____

How I like to eat it: _____

 **Ideas**

Describe a kind of bread you like. Use the details you listed on Day 4.

Look at what you wrote. Did you use any plural nouns that end in **s**? Draw a line under each one.

_____

_____

_____

_____

_____

_____

_____

_____

_____

_____

_____

_____

_____

_____

 **Ideas**   Stick to the topic to make your ideas clear.

A. Read the topic. Circle the pictures that stick to the topic.

Topic: Why I Like Blue Sky Elementary School

B. Why does the writer like Blue Sky Elementary School?
Write two reasons from the pictures.

_____

_____

 **Ideas** Stick to the topic to make your ideas clear.

A. Read each story. Cross out the detail that does <u>not</u> belong.

1. I read a good book.
   Megan is my friend.
   I took a quiz about the book.
   The quiz had ten questions.
   I answered them all correctly!

2. Trevor brings his lunch to school.
   He does not bring it on Fridays.
   He has pizza on Fridays.
   His teacher is Mrs. Sey.
   Pizza is his favorite lunch!

3. I was almost late for the bus.
   I ran out the door.
   Oh, no! I forgot my backpack.
   I went back to get it.
   My pink socks are new.

B. Add a detail to story 3. Write a telling sentence that sticks to the topic. Write a period where it belongs.

_____

_____

Ideas Stick to the topic to make your ideas clear.

A. Read the story. Cross out the two sentences that do <u>not</u> stick to the topic.

New at School

My teacher says we will have a new student. Her name is Kamry. We talked about how to help her. We can show her where to put her coat. We can sit by her in the lunchroom. She can play with us on the playground. I like to sing in music class. We can show her where to line up. She can sit with me on the bus. I like math best.

B. Write two new sentences to add to the story. Make sure that they stick to the topic. Put periods where they belong.

1. _____

_____

2. _____

_____

Daily 6-Trait Writing • EMC 6792 • © Evan-Moor Corp.

 **Ideas** Stick to the topic to make your ideas clear.

Add up the details. Think of things that make your school special.
Write them in the boxes.

Detail:

+

Detail:

+

Detail:

+

Detail:

=

Topic:

 **Ideas**

Write about what makes your school special. Use your ideas from the graphic organizer you created on Day 4.

Be sure to write a period at the end of each telling sentence.

_____

_____

_____

_____

_____

_____

_____

_____

_____

_____

_____

_____

_____

_____

 **Ideas** Choose a good topic that makes your ideas clear.

A. Draw a line under the best topic for each picture.

the nice music

Uncle Joe playing the violin

"America the Beautiful"

singing "Home on the Range"

playing music

life on a ranch

B. Write a good topic for each picture. Make your ideas clear.

_____   _____

_____   _____

_____   _____

 **Ideas** Add details to tell more about the topic.

A. Read the book report. Look for details.

Song and Dance Man
by Karen Ackerman

Song and Dance Man is a story about a grandpa. He used to be on stage many years ago. One day, his grandchildren come to visit. He takes them up to the attic. There he takes out his tap shoes, cane, and hat. He carefully shines his tap shoes and puts them on. Grandpa sings, dances, and tells funny jokes. The children don't want the show to end. They laugh and clap and shout for more. Grandpa takes a bow.

B. Write four details that the writer included.

1. _____

2. _____

3. _____

4. _____

C. Circle the capital letters in the book title on this page.

 **Ideas** Choose better details. Make sure they are important and interesting.

A. Read each pair of sentences. Circle the sentence that has interesting details.

1. A marching band came to our school on Friday.

   I saw a band.

2. They played some songs.

   The band played "twist and shout" and "circle of life."

3. After the show, we talked to the players.

   I met the players.

4. We could play the instruments.

   The drummer let me play her drum!

B. Reread the sentences above. Mark the letters that should be capitals.

C. Make this detail more interesting.

   I want to play in a band.

   _____

   _____

 **Ideas** Stick to the topic to make your ideas clear.

Tell about a musical experience you have had. Write your topic on the line.
Then write details about the experience on the drums.
Be sure the details stick to the topic.

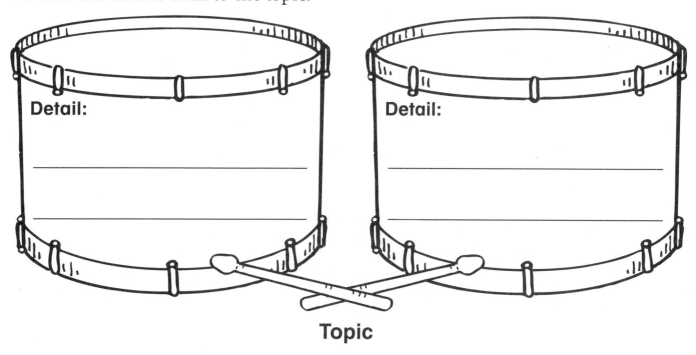

Detail:

_____

_____

Detail:

_____

_____

Topic

_____

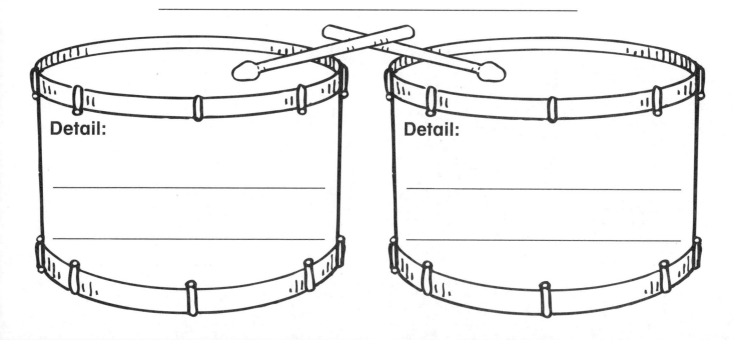

Detail:

_____

_____

Detail:

_____

_____

    Daily 6-Trait Writing • EMC 6792 • © Evan-Moor Corp.

 **Ideas**

Write a journal entry telling about a musical experience you have had. Use the topic and details you thought of on Day 4.

Be sure to capitalize the titles of songs.

Dear Journal,

_____

_____

_____

_____

_____

_____

_____

_____

_____

_____

_____

_____

_____

_____

 **Organization** Organization is putting things in the right order.

A. Read the instructions about gathering seeds. Circle the order words.

How to Gather Seeds

Would you like to study seeds? Here's how. First, ask an adult to give you an old sock. Next, put the big sock over your shoe. Then, walk through a place that has weeds. The seeds will stick to the sock. Last, take off the sock and pick off the seeds. Put them into a paper cup. You can study your seeds!

B. Draw four pictures to show how to gather seeds. Draw things in the right order.

First

Next

Then

Last

Organization Put things in the right order.

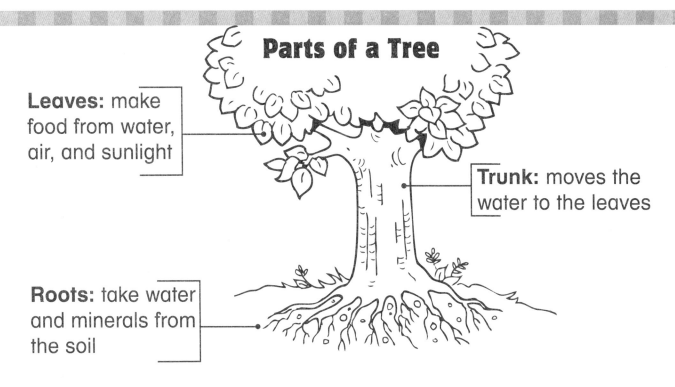

Parts of a Tree

Leaves: make food from water, air, and sunlight

Trunk: moves the water to the leaves

Roots: take water and minerals from the soil

Explain how the parts of a tree work together to get food. Put things in the right order. Finish the sentences.

First, _____

_____

Next, _____

_____

Then, _____

_____

 **Organization** Put things in the right order.

Read these sentences. Use them to complete the paragraph below.

Sentences
Then, put birdseed on a paper plate.
Next, spread peanut butter on the pine cone.
Now it's ready to hang in a tree.
First, tie a ribbon around the top of the pine cone.

Pine Cone Bird Feeder

Make a bird feeder for your bird friends. You will need

ribbon, a spoon, a paper plate, a pine cone, peanut butter, and

some birdseed. _____

_____ Leave a long piece of ribbon

for hanging. _____

_____ Fill in all the spaces. _____

_____ Roll the sticky pine

cone in the birdseed. Cover it with birdseed. _____

_____ Watch to see who comes

to eat!

 **Organization** Put things in the right order.

A. The pictures show the steps for making a leaf animal. Put them in order. Write the correct number in the corner of each picture.

B. For each step, write some words to describe it.

How to Make a Leaf Animal

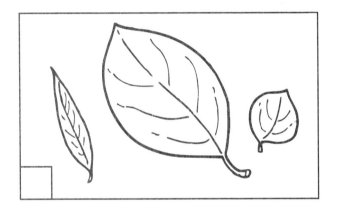

_____

_____

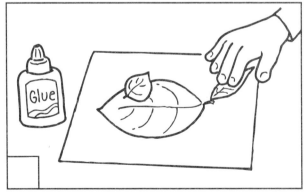

_____

_____

 **Organization**

Write complete sentences telling how to make a "leaf animal." Begin your sentences with the words **First**, **Next**, **Then**, and **Last**.

Have a partner read your writing to check for complete sentences.

_____

_____

_____

_____

_____

_____

_____

_____

_____

_____

_____

_____

Organization   A bold beginning makes the reader want to read more.

A. Read each set of beginnings. Mark an **X** by the bold beginning.

1. _____ a. My cat's four kittens were born on my birthday.

   _____ b. "Come to the barn," Alex called to me. "You have four birthday surprises!"

2. _____ a. It rained on my friend's picnic.

   _____ b. Crash! Boom! Thunder rolled as we left for the picnic.

3. _____ a. Can you imagine living over a month without sunlight?

   _____ b. Near the top of the world, the sky stays dark for a long time.

4. _____ a. Our family gave Gina a surprise.

   _____ b. Gina's face turned three shades of red when we yelled, "Surprise!"

B. Write a bold beginning for a story about your birthday. Use sound words.

_____

_____

 **Organization** A strong middle tells more about the story.

A. Read the story. Underline the middle sentences that tell more about the story. Then circle the first and last sentences. Add the missing apostrophes.

A Family Stroll

"Do you want to go for a walk?" asked my mother one morning. First, we walked past the fire station. The firefighters were cleaning their trucks. Next, we walked past my friends house. We waved to his family. Then, we took another street to my grandmothers house. She was waiting for us with a big pancake breakfast!

B. Read the beginning and ending. Then write a strong middle.

"Come quick!" yelled Maria. "You won't believe it!"

_____

_____

_____

_____

_____

That was the best school day ever!

   Daily 6-Trait Writing • EMC 6792 • © Evan-Moor Corp.

 **Organization** An excellent ending brings the story together.

A. Read the story. Fix the mistake in one sentence.
Then choose an ending from the box and circle it.

Bird Watching

One day, Grandma said, "Let's go to the park!" We packed a lunch. We found Grandma field glasses. Grandma took us to watch birds. We learned their names. We learned about nests. We found out what birds like to eat. We saw five kinds of water birds.

Possible Endings
1. **Tell what was said:** Grandma said, "You are good bird watchers."
2. **Make it funny:** Now we're bird brains!
3. **Tie it up:** Now we are expert bird watchers.

B. Write an ending for this story. Make it bring the story together.
Fix the mistake in one sentence.

Birdhouse

Grandpa picked me up after school. We made a birdhouse. I used Grandpa tools. Grandpa helped me measure and cut the wood. Next, we nailed it together. Then, we painted the birdhouse blue because that's my favorite color.

_____

_____

Organization

Write a bold beginning, a strong middle, and an excellent ending.

Tell about a fun time you've had with your family. Draw pictures to show the beginning, middle, and ending. Then write some important words to go with your pictures.

Beginning

_____

_____

_____

_____

Middle

_____

_____

_____

_____

Ending

_____

_____

_____

_____

 **Organization**

Write about a fun time you have had with your family.
Remember to add **'s** to words that show belonging.

_____

_____

_____

_____

_____

_____

_____

_____

_____

_____

_____

_____

_____

Organization Group together ideas and details to make your writing easy to read.

A. Read what Cody wrote about money.

Thanks a Million!
by Cody

What would I do with a million dollars? I would save some. I would spend some. And I would give some away. I would save some in a bank. My savings would pay for college someday. I would spend some on tickets to Disney World! Then, I would buy my dad a new truck. I would give some of it to help sick children get better. I could help a poor family build a new house. It would be fun to have a million dollars.

B. Find the ideas and details Cody grouped together.
Draw a line under the details about saving.
Draw two lines under the details about spending.
Circle the details about giving.

C. Draw a new detail for Cody.
Write **save, spend,** or **give**
to go with your picture.

_____

 Daily 6-Trait Writing • EMC 6792 • © Evan-Moor Corp.

Organization Group together ideas and details.

A. Read each sentence. Think about the details in it.
Write **1** or **2** for the picture it goes with.
Then write the missing end mark.

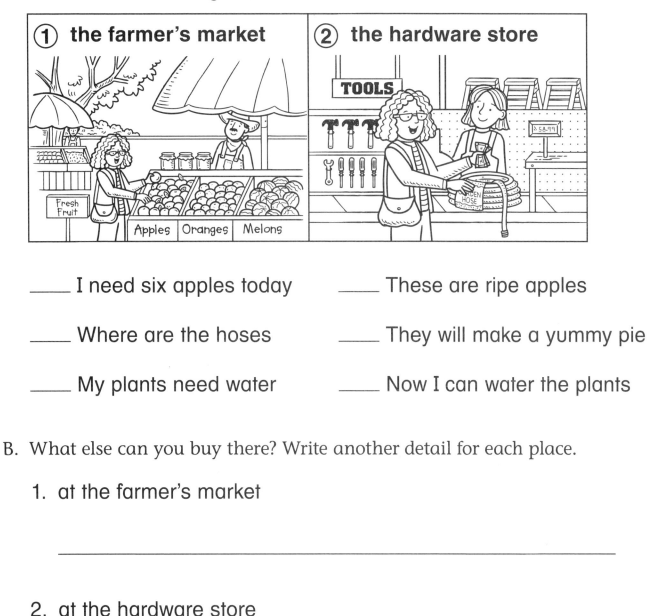

① **the farmer's market**   ② **the hardware store**

TOOLS

Fresh Fruit

Apples | Oranges | Melons

_____ I need six apples today   _____ These are ripe apples

_____ Where are the hoses   _____ They will make a yummy pie

_____ My plants need water   _____ Now I can water the plants

B. What else can you buy there? Write another detail for each place.

1. at the farmer's market

_____

2. at the hardware store

_____

Organization Group together ideas and details.

Read the story and the sentences in the box.
Write each sentence where it belongs in the story.
Add the correct end mark to each sentence.

Sentences
They go clink
Then we will go to the game store
It is a funny pink pig
Which game should I buy

My Piggy Bank

My grandpa gave me a bank. _____

I like to drop my shiny coins into it. _____

Soon, I'll have enough for a new game. _____

_____

_____

_____

 **Organization**   Group together ideas and details.

A. Imagine you could design your own paper money.
   What would it look like? Write details about your bill.

My bill has these words and numbers:

1. _____

2. _____

3. _____

My bill has pictures of: My bill has these colors:

1. _____   1. _____

2. _____   2. _____

3. _____   3. _____

B. Now draw your bill.

 **Organization**

Use your ideas and details from Day 4 to write a description of your new paper money.

Be sure to use correct end marks.

_____

_____

_____

_____

_____

_____

_____

_____

_____

_____

_____

_____

_____

_____

_____

 **Organization** | Ideas and details can be grouped by how they are the same or different.

A. Some sentences tell how two things are the **same**.
   Draw a line under the two things that are the same.

   Soccer and baseball are both team sports.

B. Some sentences tell how two things are **different**.
   Draw a line under the two things that are different.

   In soccer you kick the ball, but in baseball you hit it.

C. Read the sentence that tells about each picture. Circle **same** or **different** to show what the sentence is telling.

They both play baseball.

Tyler is a Cub, but Jerome is a Blue Jay.

same   different

same   different

D. Write a sentence that tells how the boys above are different.

_____

_____

 **Organization** Group by how things are different.

A. How are swimming and ice-skating different?
Find words in the box that tell how they are different.
Write the words in the chart.

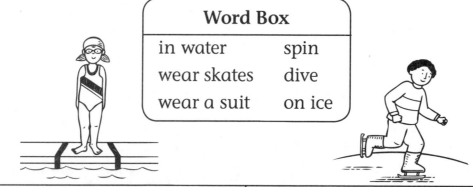

Word Box

in water	spin
wear skates	dive
wear a suit	on ice

Swimming	Ice-Skating
pool	rink

B. Complete the sentence that tells how swimming and
ice-skating are different.

You swim in a pool _____ you ice-skate at a rink.

Organization

Group by how things are the same and different.

A. Read the Venn diagram. It tells how basketball and hockey are the same and different.

Basketball
a ball
5 players
run
basket

Both
players shoot to score
teams
players pass
have a net

Hockey
a puck
6 players
skate
goal

B. Finish the sentence to tell how basketball and hockey are the **same**.

Both basketball and hockey _____

_____

C. Write a sentence to tell how basketball and hockey are **different**.

_____

_____

 **Organization**

Group by how things are the same and different.

Complete the Venn diagram. Write how a baseball and a basketball are the same and different.

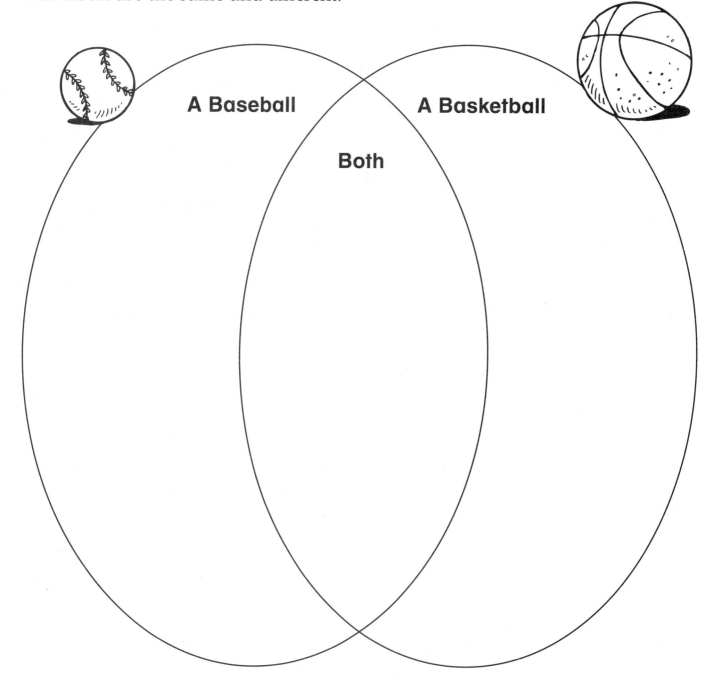

A Baseball

Both

A Basketball

   Daily 6-Trait Writing • EMC 6792 • © Evan-Moor Corp.

 **Organization**

Use your ideas from Day 4 to write sentences that tell how a baseball and a basketball are the same and different.

Be sure to use a comma and the word **but** correctly.

_____

_____

_____

_____

_____

_____

_____

_____

_____

_____

_____

_____

_____

_____

Organization Organization is putting things in the right order.

A. Read how to make a puppet.

Ugly Duckling Puppet

Make a puppet to tell the story. First, cut two pieces of paper the same size. Next, draw the ugly duckling on one. Then, draw the beautiful swan on the other. Last, glue the pictures to a craft stick. Glue them on back to back. Use one side at a time when you tell the story.

B. Look at the pictures. Write an order word and an action word to describe which step each picture shows.

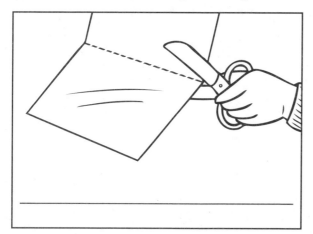

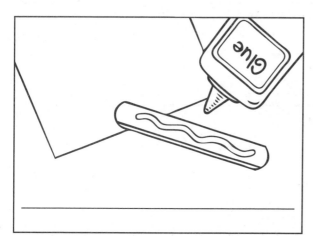

Daily 6-Trait Writing • EMC 6792 • © Evan-Moor Corp.

 **Organization** A story should have organization.

Write a bold beginning, a strong middle, and an excellent ending.

The Ugly Duckling

_____

_____

_____

_____

_____

_____

_____

_____

_____

Organization Group together ideas and details.

A. Read the paragraph and the sentences in the box.
Write each detail sentence where it belongs.

Sentences
It cracks open the egg.
The feathers are also wet and sticky.
The dull gray feathers will turn to snow white.

The Real Ugly Duckling

A cygnet is a name for a baby swan. A cygnet are a bird, so

it begins life inside an egg. When it is ready to be born, the cygnet

uses its beak. _____

A newborn cygnet's feathers is gray. _____

_____ As the cygnet

grows older, its gray feathers will change color. _____

_____

_____

B. Read the paragraph again. Use proofreading marks to correct
the use of **is** and **are**.

 **Organization** Group by how things are the same or different.

What did you look like as a baby?
What do you look like now?
Fill in the diagram.

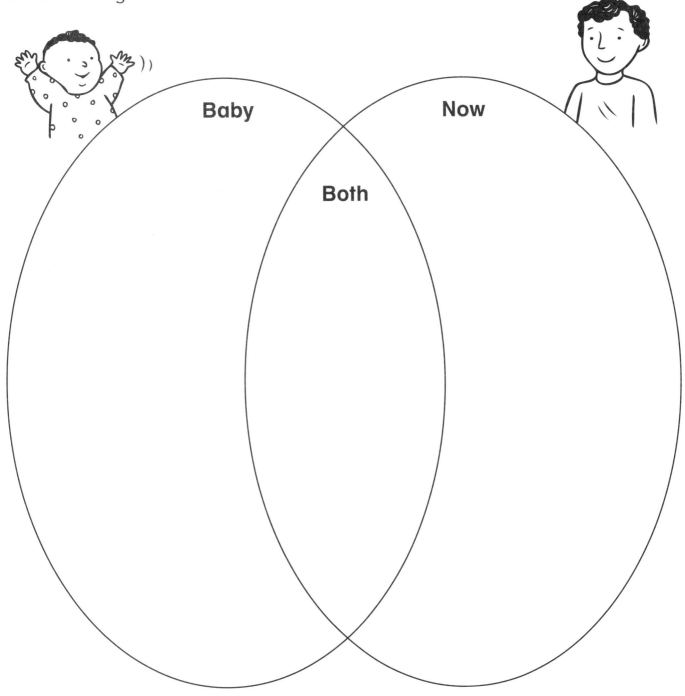

Baby

Now

Both

 **Organization**

Use your diagram from Day 4 to write sentences about how you looked as a baby and how you look now.

Be sure to use **is** and **are** correctly.

_____

_____

_____

_____

_____

_____

_____

_____

_____

_____

_____

_____

_____

_____

Daily 6-Trait Writing • EMC 6792 • © Evan-Moor Corp.

 **Word Choice** Strong verbs make your writing sparkle.

A. Look at the pictures. Circle the stronger verb for each picture.

dance   twirl

called   said

hit   bump

wiggle   move

trot   go

eat   gobble

B. Underline the verb in each sentence. Then circle the plural noun that is doing the action.

1. My feet tap to the music.

2. The men leap across the floor.

3. The women twirl around the room.

 **Word Choice**

Strong verbs make your ideas clear.
Verbs such as **go** and **get** are not clear.

A. Read the sentences. Write the stronger verb in each sentence.

1. This tractor won't _____.
   (go / start)

2. I want to _____ down to the barn.
   (go / ride)

3. We have to _____ some hay.
   (carry / get)

4. The horses _____ quickly.
   (gallop / go)

5. Soon, we have to _____.
   (go / leave)

6. The horses _____ into the trailer.
   (step / get)

7. The geese want to _____.
   (follow / go)

8. The mice _____ away.
   (go / scamper)

B. The plurals of some nouns have special spellings. Use the words on this page to write the plural forms.

1. More than one goose flies. _____

2. More than one foot stamps. _____

3. More than one mouse scampers. _____

Word Choice

Strong verbs make your writing interesting. Use verbs that aren't "tired."

A. Read the story below. The underlined words are "tired" verbs. Find a stronger verb to use instead. Write each tired verb next to a strong verb in the chart.

At the Fair

The fair had a watermelon-eating contest. My brother and I <u>went</u> early and entered it. We <u>ate</u> our watermelon. Then, my tooth <u>came</u> loose! Out it <u>came</u>! I had to stop eating. My brother never stopped, though. He kept chomping away. He <u>got</u> first prize!

Strong Verbs	Tired Verbs
gobbled	_____
wiggled	_____
arrived	_____
won	_____
popped	_____

B. Write a sentence about teeth. Use a strong verb from this page, or use your own.

_____

C. Write the plurals for **tooth** and **child** to complete the sentence.

How many _____ have the _____ lost?

Word Choice Use strong verbs in your writing.

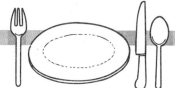

Think about lunchtime at your school.
How many different ways can you eat something?
Read the verbs for **eat**. Draw a picture of a food for each one.
Then write and draw three more strong verbs.

munch	gobble	nibble

 Daily 6-Trait Writing • EMC 6792 • © Evan-Moor Corp.

Word Choice

Describe what lunchtime is like at your school. Use strong verbs to tell how kids eat and act.

Some plural nouns have special spellings. Be sure to spell these words correctly.

_____

_____

_____

_____

_____

_____

_____

_____

_____

_____

_____

_____

_____

_____

 **Word Choice**

Adverbs describe action.
Some adverbs tell **how**.

A. Circle the adverb that goes with the picture.

sing   loudly   neatly

run   swiftly   tightly

act   carefully   kindly

talk   secretly   finally

B. Finish each sentence with an adverb that describes the action.
Underline the word that names a day of the week.

1. Kyra ran _____ in the race on Friday.

2. Tim sang _____ in music class on Tuesday.

Daily 6-Trait Writing • EMC 6792 • © Evan-Moor Corp.

 **Word Choice**

Describe action with adverbs that tell **how**, **when**, or **where**.

A. Look at the picture. Write the pair of words that makes sense in each sentence. Circle the adverb.

A Snow Day

Word Box	
closed today	snowed heavily
play outside	always go

1. On Sunday, it _____ _____.

2. We _____ _____ to school on Monday.

3. But school is _____ _____.

4. Mom said we can _____ _____!

B. On what days do you go to school? Write the days of the week.

_____

_____

 **Word Choice** Describe action with adverbs.

A. Use the adverbs to describe the action in the picture.
Write two sentences about the picture.

A Summer Day

brightly

quietly

swiftly

nearby

proudly

happily

carefully

today

outside

1. _____

_____

2. _____

_____

B. Mark the words that need a capital letter.

1. On wednesday I rode my bike carefully.

2. Will you meet me outside on friday?

 **Word Choice** Describe action with adverbs.

What is your favorite day of the week? Complete the web to tell what you do on that day.

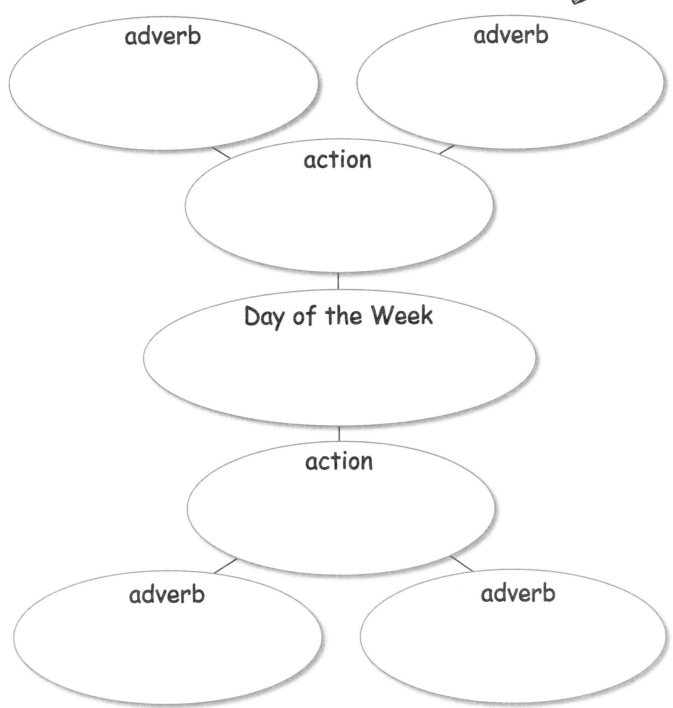

Word Choice

Write a description of what you do on your favorite day of the week. Use your web from Day 4.

Be sure to capitalize the day of the week you are writing about.

_____

_____

_____

_____

_____

_____

_____

_____

_____

_____

_____

_____

_____

_____

 **Word Choice** Describing words tell more about people, places, and things.

A. Write each describing word under the correct picture.

Word Box			
tiny	terrible	light	graceful
scaly	spiky	huge	feathery

_____

_____

_____

_____

_____

_____

_____

_____

B. Write your own describing word for each picture.

_____   _____

Word Choice

Adjectives describe people, places, and things.

A. Complete each sentence with the adjective.

1. Here are the _____ rocks.
    (under / red)

2. We are hunting for _____ fossils.
    (hidden / pick)

3. We filled _____ buckets.
    (two / think)

4. Isn't this rock _____?
    (almost / shiny)

5. There aren't any _____ fossils here.
    (big / work)

6. We haven't seen _____ dinosaur bones yet.
    (dig / old)

B. Circle three contractions in the sentences above.
   Write the two words each one stands for on the lines.

_____   _____   _____

 **Word Choice**   Adjectives describe people, places, and things.

A. Read the friendly letter. Circle the adjectives the writer used.

> June 15, 2010
>
> Dear Shelby,
>
>   Wouldn't you like to see the new Science Center? It has giant dinosaurs. They make loud noises. They have scaly skin. They seem almost real! I can't wait for your visit. We can pretend to be dinosaur trackers. I'll see you soon!
>
>   Your cousin,
>
>   Claire

B. Find a sentence with an adjective in the letter above. Change the adjective to a new one. Write the new sentence.

_____

_____

C. Find the contractions for these words in the letter. Write the contractions.

would not   _____

can not   _____

I will   _____

 **Word Choice**

Adjectives describe how something looks, feels, sounds, tastes, or smells.

Pretend you have tasted a new snack called Dinosaur Munch. Think of words to describe how it looks, feels, sounds, tastes, and smells. Write two or more adjectives in each bag.

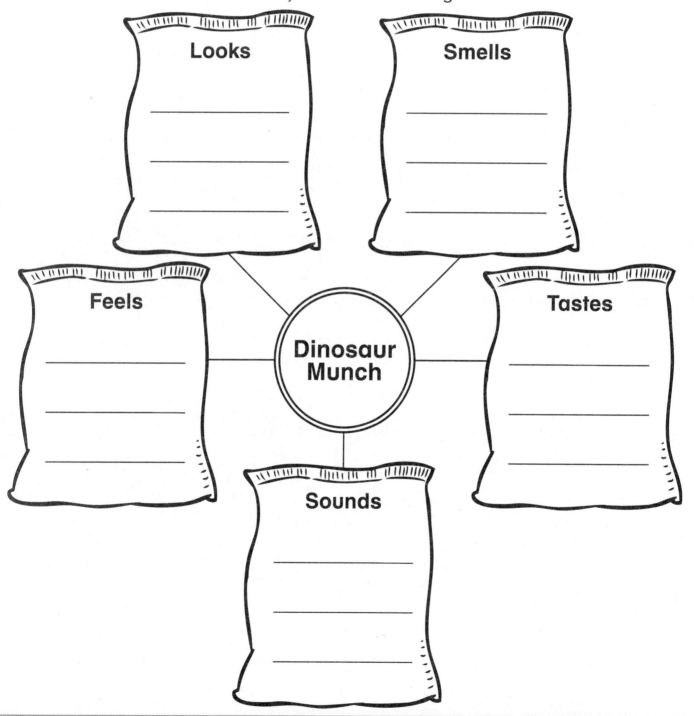

Daily 6-Trait Writing • EMC 6792 • © Evan-Moor Corp.

 **Word Choice**

Write a letter to a friend, telling him or her about your new favorite snack—Dinosaur Munch. Use your adjectives from Day 4.

Be sure to spell contractions correctly.

_____

_____

_____

_____

_____

_____

_____

_____

_____

_____

_____

_____

_____

 **Word Choice** Exact nouns paint a picture for the reader.

A. Mark an **X** by the sentence that uses an exact noun.

1. ☐ My neighbor has a **poodle** named Wally.

   ☐ Does he have a **dog** named Wally?

2. ☐ Jordan wears new **shoes**.

   ☐ Did you see his new **sneakers**?

3. ☐ Miss Rosa lives in the **palace** on the hill.

   ☐ Does Miss Rosa live in the **house** on the hill?

4. ☐ I took **flowers** to Grandma.

   ☐ Do you know Grandma loves **daisies**?

5. ☐ She found a **bug**.

   ☐ Where did she find the **grasshopper**?

B. Circle the question marks on this page.

Word Choice Use exact nouns to help the reader picture what you mean.

A. Read the nouns in the word box. Write the exact noun that names each picture. Cross out the weak nouns.

Word Box				
tree	rancher	house	water	farmhouse
man	animal	pony	pond	oak

B. Write one question about the picture.

_____

_____

 **Word Choice** Use exact nouns instead of weak nouns.

A. Circle the weak noun in each sentence. Then rewrite the sentence using an exact noun from the word box.

Word Box	
maple	rocking chair
cabin	apartment
palm	porch swing

1. Jessie's favorite place is her home.

_____

_____

2. A huge tree grows next to it.

_____

_____

3. She likes to read in her chair.

_____

_____

B. Write a question. Use an exact noun from the word box.

_____

_____

Word Choice Use exact nouns. Choose the right word for what you want to say.

A. Look at the picture of the castle.
Write exact nouns to describe what you see in each room.

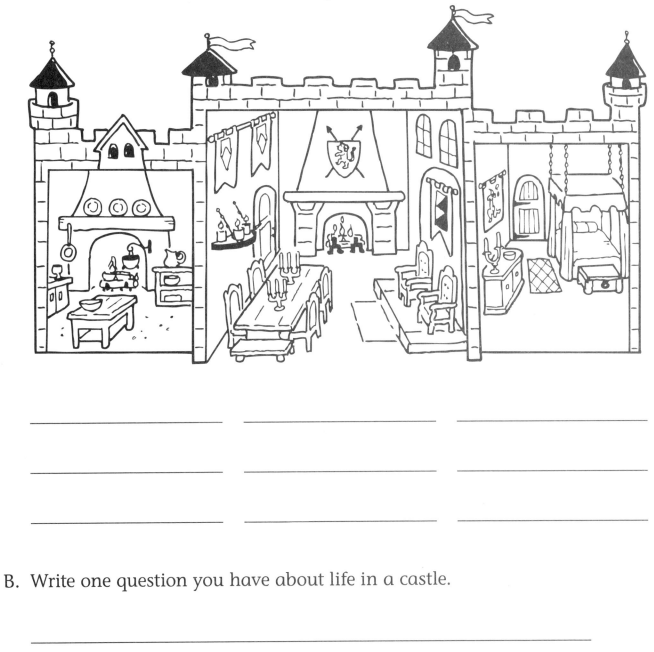

_____   _____   _____

_____   _____   _____

_____   _____   _____

B. Write one question you have about life in a castle.

_____

_____

Word Choice

Write a description of the castle pictured on page 71. Use some of the exact nouns you wrote.

Finish the question at the top of this page. Be sure to place a question mark at the end.

<u>What is in the   </u>

_____

_____

_____

_____

_____

_____

_____

_____

_____

_____

_____

Word Choice Use strong verbs to make your ideas clear.

A. Circle the stronger verb that could be used to tell about each book.

look   search

go   travel

discover   see

explain   tell

think   imagine

fly   soar

B. Underline the word that comes before **seen** in each sentence.

1. Mari has seen a travel show.

2. The boys have seen a book about rockets.

3. I have seen him before.

 **Word Choice** Use adverbs to describe the action in a sentence.

A. Write an adverb to describe the action in each sentence.

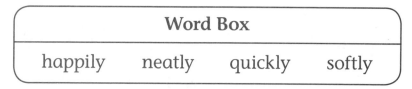

Word Box
happily   neatly   quickly   softly

1. I have seen Carlos write with care. He writes _____.

2. I saw a sign in the library. It said we must speak _____.

3. The students have seen the winner of the poetry contest.

   She smiles _____.

4. Ben has seen the clock. He _____ puts away his book.

B. Choose two words from the word box. Write a sentence using each one.

1. _____

2. _____

C. Circle **saw** and **seen** in Activity A. Then complete the rules below for using the words.

   Rule: Use **have** or **has** in front of _____.

   Rule: Use _____ by itself.

 **Word Choice** — Use adjectives to describe people, places, and things.

A. Read the paragraph Amy wrote about her school. Circle the adjectives.

My school is in a small town on a quiet street. Many people make my school a happy place. Kind, smart teachers help students learn. Cooks prepare hot, tasty lunches. Cleaners scrub the floors to keep them shiny.

B. Write two sentences to add to Amy's paragraph. Use at least one adjective in each sentence.

1. _____

   _____

2. _____

   _____

C. Use proofreading marks to fix the sentences.

1. Matt seen the new library.

2. Megan and Abby have saw it, too.

3. I seen it on my way to school.

Word Choice Use exact nouns to tell just what you want to say.

Think about your school.
Fill in the chart with exact nouns.

Weak Noun	Exact Noun
school	
class	
teacher	
book	
friend	
meal	
food	

Daily 6-Trait Writing • EMC 6792 • © Evan-Moor Corp.

Word Choice

Write a description of your school. Include exact nouns and strong verbs, adjectives, and adverbs. Use your ideas from Day 4.

Be sure to use **saw** and **seen** correctly.

_____

_____

_____

_____

_____

_____

_____

_____

_____

_____

_____

_____

_____

_____

_____

 **Sentence Fluency**

A sentence forms a complete thought.
It has a naming part and a telling part.

A. The naming part of a sentence names someone or something.
Look at the picture and read the words. Then write a naming part
for the sentence.

_____ is in
a big jug.

_____ baked
muffins for Vanessa and me.

B. The telling part of a sentence tells what someone or something does
or is. Look at the picture and read the words. Then write a telling part
for the sentence.

My baby sister _____

_____ .

Mrs. Rossi and I _____

_____ .

C. Circle the words **I** and **me**.

1. Rose and I write the answers on the board.

2. The teacher hands the rulers to Rose and me.

 Daily 6-Trait Writing • EMC 6792 • © Evan-Moor Corp.

 **Sentence Fluency**   Write sentences with naming parts and telling parts.

A. A sentence has a naming part and a telling part.
   Read the sentence parts. Write them in the chart.

buy the treats	I	the bake sale
choose a brownie	cost 25 cents	will raise money
the cookies	people	

Naming Parts	Telling Parts

B. Use a naming part from the chart to write a complete sentence.

_____

C. Use a telling part from the chart to write a complete sentence.

_____

D. Write **I** or **me** to complete the sentences.

   1. Grandpa pours milk for Rico and _____.

   2. Rico and _____ drink the milk.

Sentence Fluency

Write sentences with naming parts and telling parts.

A. Write four sentences about the picture. Circle the naming parts. Underline the telling parts.

Toys for Sale!

1. _____

2. _____

3. _____

4. _____

B. Finish the sentences about yourself and a friend. Put your friend's name first. Remember to use **I** and **me** correctly.

1. _____ and _____ went to the school fair.

2. Dad bought a toy for _____ and _____.

Use naming parts and telling parts to plan sentences.

Think about what happens at a bake sale. Complete the chart with naming parts and telling parts.

Bake Sale

What to Buy	What to Do	Who Is There

Sentence Fluency

Describe a bake sale. Use the naming parts and telling parts you wrote on Day 4 to form sentences.

Be sure to use the words **I** and **me** correctly.

_____

_____

_____

_____

_____

_____

_____

_____

_____

_____

_____

_____

_____

_____

Daily 6-Trait Writing • EMC 6792 • © Evan-Moor Corp.

 **Sentence Fluency**   Longer sentences make your writing flow smoothly.

A. Read the pairs of sentences. Draw a line under the words that were added in the second sentence.

Have you watched an ant?

Have you ever watched an ant at work?

Ants live in a group.

Ants live in a group called a colony.

I got an ant farm.

For my birthday last year, I got an ant farm.

Ants are fun to watch!

Ants are busy, strong, and fun to watch!

B. Circle the commas in the last sentence above. List three things the sentence tells about ants.

_____   _____   _____

Sentence Fluency

Add words that tell **when**, **where**, and **how** to write longer sentences.

A. Read the sentences. Underline the words that tell **when**, **where**, or **how**.

1. (where) The bees were buzzing in the roses.

2. (when) Every afternoon, a lizard visits the garden.

3. (how) The cricket chirps over and over.

B. Read the sentences. Add words that tell **when**, **where**, or **how** to make the sentences longer.

1. The bees are working. (where)

_____

2. I heard a cricket chirp. (when)

_____

3. A butterfly flew away. (how)

_____

4. The sun shines. (when)

_____

 Daily 6-Trait Writing • EMC 6792 • © Evan-Moor Corp.

Sentence Fluency

Use lists to write longer sentences.

A. Read the sentences. Add commas to the lists.

1. The beetle uses its mouth for cutting biting and chewing.

2. Grasshoppers crickets and some spiders are good jumpers.

3. Ants bees and wasps live in colonies.

4. Some butterflies are called skippers blues or coppers.

5. Caterpillars make cocoons turn into butterflies and fly away.

B. Write a sentence listing three insects you like or do not like.
Use commas.

_____

_____

C. Write a sentence telling three things that some insects do.
Use commas.

_____

_____

Sentence Fluency

Write longer sentences.

Here are some sentences for a story. Write words and phrases that you might use to make the sentences longer.

June Bug had a picnic. (**where**)

1. __by the lake__

2. _____

3. _____

They sang. (**how**)

1. __along with Cricket's fiddle__

2. _____

3. _____

They danced. (**when**)

1. __that evening__

2. _____

3. _____

June Bug's Picnic

Everyone ate. (**what**)

1. __pie, watermelon, and salad__

2. _____

3. _____

 **Sentence Fluency**

Write a story entitled "June Bug's Picnic." Use the sentences and words you wrote in the web on Day 4.

Be sure to use commas to separate items in a list.

_____

_____

_____

_____

_____

_____

_____

_____

_____

_____

_____

_____

_____

_____

_____

Sentence Fluency

A run-on sentence is two sentences joined together. Fix a run-on sentence with a comma and the word **and**.

A. Read each pair of sentences. Mark an **X** next to the run-on sentence.

1. ___ We got a new mouse her name is Tiny.

   ___ We got a new mouse, and her name is Tiny.

2. ___ We bought a wheel for Tiny, and the vet gave us food.

   ___ We bought a wheel for Tiny the vet gave us food.

3. ___ She eats from a bowl she drinks from a bottle.

   ___ She eats from a bowl. She drinks from a bottle.

4. ___ I feed her every day, and I let her out to play.

   ___ I feed her every day I let her out to play.

B. Revise these run-on sentences. Rewrite each one, using a period or a comma and **and**.

1. Tiny is small she has white fur.

   _____

2. She plays in her wheel she squeaks a lot.

   _____

   _____

    Daily 6-Trait Writing • EMC 6792 • © Evan-Moor Corp.

Sentence Fluency

Break a rambling sentence into smaller sentences.

A. Use proofreading marks to break the run-on sentences into smaller sentences.

   1. A drum is loud and a trumpet is loud but a violin is soft and a piano is soft, too.

   2. The horn plays and then the trumpet plays and then the singers sing.

B. Rewrite each run-on sentence. Turn it into two or more smaller sentences.

   1. Some music is fast and some music is slow and some music is in between and I like any kind.

   _____

   _____

   2. The band played a funny song and then they played a sad song and then they took a break and then they played a loud song and then the concert was over.

   _____

   _____

   _____

   _____

 **Sentence Fluency**   Fix run-on and rambling sentences.

A. Read this letter. Underline the run-on and rambling sentences.

Dear Justin,

   Yesterday I went to the Science Museum it was fun!
We saw ladybugs living in bamboo and then we ate lunch
in the park, and then we got on the bus. I love field trips
the Science Museum is my favorite.

                                    Your pal,
                                    Olivia

B. Rewrite Olivia's letter. Fix the run-on and rambling sentences.

Dear Justin,

_____

_____

_____

_____

_____

                                    Your pal,
                                    Olivia

    Daily 6-Trait Writing • EMC 6792 • © Evan-Moor Corp.

Sentence Fluency

Avoid run-on and rambling sentences.

Think of a fun place you've been to. Fill in the web with five details about what you saw and did there.

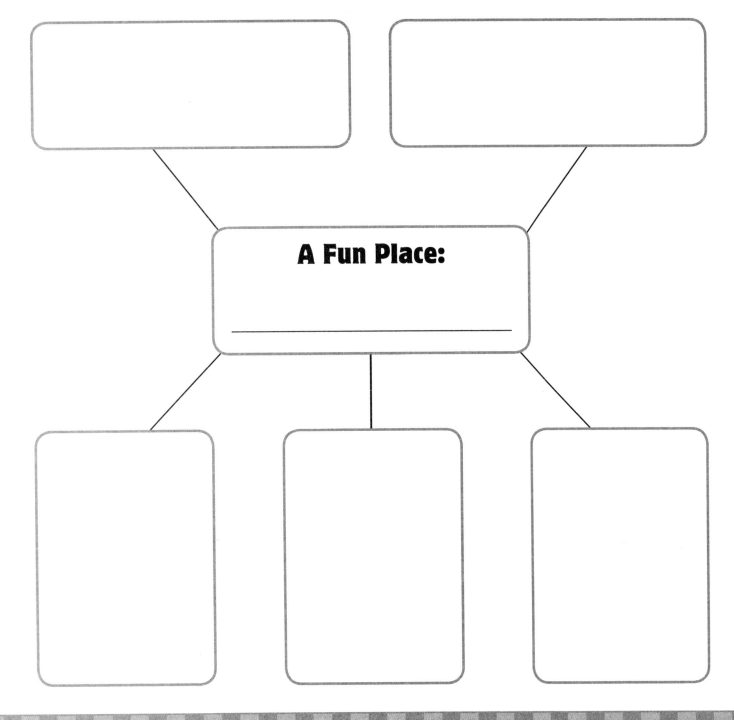

A Fun Place:
_____

Sentence Fluency

Write a letter to a friend telling about a fun place you've been to. Use the details you wrote on Day 4.

Be careful not to write run-on or rambling sentences.

_____

_____

_____

_____

_____

_____

_____

_____

_____

_____

_____

_____

_____

_____

 **Sentence Fluency** Combine choppy sentences to make your writing flow.

A. Rewrite these short sentences as one smooth sentence.

1. Frida Frog eats bugs. Freddy Frog eats bugs.

   _____

2. Freddy Frog has webbed feet. He swims with his feet.

   _____

3. Frida lives in a pond. Freddy lives in the pond, too.

   _____

4. Frida has long back legs. Frida has short front legs.

   _____

B. Circle the comma and the joining word in these compound sentences.

1. We walk to the park, and we sit by the pond.

2. The waterlily smells sweet, but the mud is stinky.

3. We can watch the ducks dive, or we can follow the frog.

Sentence Fluency

Combine choppy sentences with a comma and **and**, **but**, or **or**.

Combine the sentences into compound sentences.

1. We saw a fish. We didn't see a turtle.

   _____

2. We can wade in the water. We can eat lunch.

   _____

3. I like to play in the mud. I like to count the ducks.

   _____

   _____

4. Baby geese stay with their parents. Baby turtles leave.

   _____

   _____

5. A dragonfly begins its life underwater. It ends its life in the air.

   _____

   _____

                     Daily 6-Trait Writing • EMC 6792 • © Evan-Moor Corp.

Sentence Fluency

Combine choppy sentences.

Read the paragraph. Underline the choppy sentences. Combine them to write new sentences on the lines.

The Life Cycle of a Moth

All moths change as they grow. A caterpillar hatches from an egg. It eats. It grows. Then the caterpillar spins a cocoon around its body. The caterpillar changes. It changes into an adult. The adult moth climbs out of the cocoon. Its wings dry. It flies away.

1. _____

_____

2. _____

_____

3. _____

_____

Sentence Fluency

Make your writing flow.

Write short sentences or phrases to describe each stage in the life cycle of a frog.

The Life Cycle of a Frog

Sentence Fluency

Describe the life cycle of a frog. Combine the sentences and phrases you wrote on Day 4.

Be sure to form compound sentences correctly with a comma and a joining word.

_____

_____

_____

_____

_____

_____

_____

_____

_____

_____

_____

_____

_____

_____

Sentence Fluency

A sentence has a naming part and a telling part.

A. Read each sentence. Circle the naming part.
Underline the telling part.

In the Rainforest

1. Spider monkeys live in the highest treetops.

2. A spotted butterfly hides in the trees.

3. Rainforest bats hunt for food at night.

4. Harpy eagles build huge nests in the tallest trees.

B. Write a telling part to complete the sentences.

1. _A colorful parrot_ _____

2. _A striped tiger_ _____

3. _A crocodile_ _____

C. Circle the comparing words in these sentences.
Look for **er** and **est**.

1. A monkey is faster than a sloth.

2. Three-toed sloths are the slowest mammals in the rainforest.

Daily 6-Trait Writing • EMC 6792 • © Evan-Moor Corp.

 **Sentence Fluency** Write longer sentences.

A. Read the sentences. Add phrases from the box that tell **when**, **where**, or **how**. Write the longer sentences.

Word Box	
in the treetops	in the evening
with their legs stretched out	

1. Flying squirrels climb up the trees. (when)

   _____

   _____

2. The squirrels look for food. (where)

   _____

   _____

3. They glide through the air. (how)

   _____

   _____

B. Add commas where they are needed in the sentences below.

   1. Flying squirrels eat leaves shoots and nuts.

   2. Insects birds and bats help to spread seeds.

 Fix run-on and choppy sentences.

A. Read the paragraph aloud.

Life in the Rainforest

My family lives in a small village and it is in the rainforest and our house is near a river. The house is round many families live in it together. We work together, too. We grow crops. We hunt.

B. Fix the run-on and choppy sentences. Rewrite the paragraph.

_____

_____

_____

_____

_____

_____

C. Complete each sentence with a comparing word. Use **er** or **est**.

1. A cobra is _____ than a viper.
(long)

2. The kapok tree is the _____ tree in the rainforest.
(tall)

Sentence Fluency

Make your writing flow.

Pretend you went to the rainforest. Write short sentences or phrases to describe your adventure.

Why I was there:

How I felt:

My Rainforest Adventure

What I saw:

What happened:

Sentence Fluency

Use your ideas from Day 4 to write about your rainforest adventure! Try not to use run-ons or choppy sentences.

Use at least one comparing word with **er** or **est**.

_____

_____

_____

_____

_____

_____

_____

_____

_____

_____

_____

_____

_____

_____

Daily 6-Trait Writing • EMC 6792 • © Evan-Moor Corp.

 **Voice** — Formal language is different from informal language.

A. Read the letter and e-mail message. Think about which one uses **formal** language and which one uses **informal** language. Answer the questions.

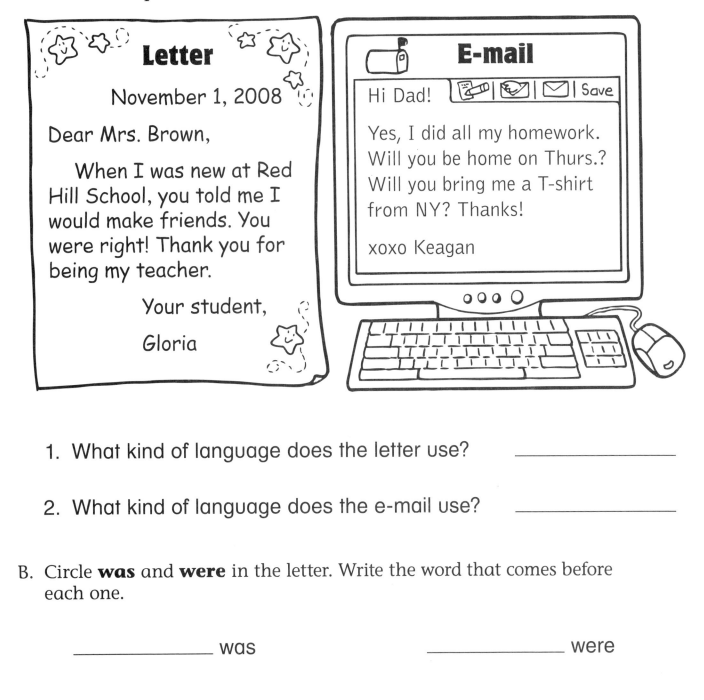

Letter

November 1, 2008

Dear Mrs. Brown,

When I was new at Red Hill School, you told me I would make friends. You were right! Thank you for being my teacher.

Your student,

Gloria

E-mail

Hi Dad!

Yes, I did all my homework. Will you be home on Thurs.? Will you bring me a T-shirt from NY? Thanks!

xoxo Keagan

1. What kind of language does the letter use? _____

2. What kind of language does the e-mail use? _____

B. Circle **was** and **were** in the letter. Write the word that comes before each one.

_____ was   _____ were

 **Voice** Use formal language in a report.

A. Read what Drew wrote in his report about a covered bridge.

A Bridge in the Country

Last fall, our family drove to the country. There were many colorful trees. Their leaves were red, orange, and gold. We also went to see White's Bridge. This is an old covered bridge. You might wonder why a bridge has a roof. It is because the bridge is made of wood, and wood rots if it gets wet. The roof is there to keep the wood dry.

B. Help Drew finish his report. Choose two sentences from below that use formal language. Write them on the lines.

The roof must have worked.   Check it out sometime.

The bridge is over 100 years old!   It was very cool.

_____

_____

C. Write **was** or **were** to complete each sentence.

1. We _____ in the country.

2. The trip _____ fun.

3. I'm glad you _____ there.

 **Voice** Use informal language in a postcard.

Read each postcard. Underline the sentence that sounds more formal. Rewrite it to sound informal.

Hi Miguel,

   Camping at the lake is so cool. We get up early and build a fire. Then, we help Mother prepare the morning meal. After that, we get to swim all day long.

             Your friend,
             Cole

_____

_____

_____

_____

Hey Cole!

   We drove over a huge bridge in Michigan! It's one of the longest in the whole world. Dad says it's 5 miles long. People call it the "Mighty Mac" because it's super-big. I do not know the exact height of the bridge, however. It was so awesome!

           See you soon,
           Miguel

_____

_____

_____

_____

 **Voice**   Use formal and informal language.

Plan a report about a special landmark in your area.
Use informal language to complete the graphic organizer.

Where is it?

Why is it important?

Landmark:

What does it look like?

How was it built or made?

 **Voice**

Write a report about a landmark in your area. Use formal language and the information you found on Day 4.

Be sure to use **was** and **were** correctly.

_____

_____

_____

_____

_____

_____

_____

_____

_____

_____

_____

_____

_____

_____

 **Voice**

Your writing has a style.
What you write can be funny or silly.

A. Read the paragraph. Then answer the question.

Rub a Dub Dub

How do you like your bath? Do you like a tub full of bubbles? Maybe you float with your rubber ducky. Animals enjoy their baths, too. Pigs love mud baths. Look at a pig in mud. You'll see a happy animal. Have you ever seen an elephant take a shower? Elephants use their trunks. They spray water onto their backs. Don't get in the way! You could get a shower, too. Birds have it easy. They just find a puddle and splash, splash, splash! Which kind of bath would you enjoy?

In what style was the paragraph written?

_____ Serious _____ Funny, silly _____ Exciting

B. Which group of sentences fits the style used in the paragraph? Mark the answer with an **X**.

_____ 1. Would you roll in the dust to get clean? That's what a horse does! You see, a horse doesn't fit into a bathtub.

_____ 2. To give your dog a bath, first brush it. This will get rid of loose hair. Use dog shampoo. It is good for your dog's skin.

C. Find each of these words in the story. Write the word that comes before it.

_____ pig _____ elephant _____ puddle

Daily 6-Trait Writing • EMC 6792 • © Evan-Moor Corp.

 **Voice** Your writing can have a serious style.

A. Read this formal letter. Then answer the question.

January 6, 2010

Dear Dr. Hall,

Thank you for talking to our class. I had never met an animal scientist before. I am glad your zoo is helping to save the giant pandas. I learned many things about them. Pandas eat mostly bamboo. A baby panda is helpless when it is born. Its mother takes good care of it. I hope you will find more new ways to help them.

Your friend,
Maya

In what style was the letter written?

_____ Serious   _____ Funny, silly   _____ Exciting

B. Maya wants to be an animal scientist. Finish this sentence to put in her letter. Write it in the same style as the letter.

<u>Someday, I hope</u> _____

_____

C. Which word should come before each phrase below? Write **a** or **an**.

_____ mother bear   _____ angry baby

 **Voice** Your writing can have an exciting style.

A. Owen wrote a book report in an exciting style. He wants to get others to read the book. Read the report and listen for Owen's voice.

Book Report

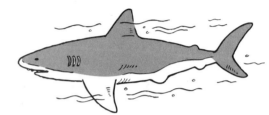

Name: Owen
Book Title: <u>Hungry, Hungry Sharks!</u>
Author: Joanna Cole

   If you like sharks, this book is for you! <u>Hungry, Hungry Sharks!</u> is a nonfiction book. The facts I read made my mouth drop open. There are more than 300 kinds of sharks! Some are as small as your hand. Others are as long as a bus! Sharks use up thousands of teeth every year. This is because they eat so much. Most sharks eat fish, but some eat little shrimp or giant whales. Some have even eaten bottles, drums, and cans! I never knew sharks ate so many things. They really are very hungry!

B. Draw a line under two sentences that might make the reader excited about the book.

C. Think about an exciting book you have read. Write two sentences that show your excitement about the book. Use **a** or **an** correctly.

1. _____

   _____

2. _____

   _____

 **Voice**   Write in a funny, serious, or exciting style.

Think of an interesting animal. What makes it interesting?
Write your ideas in the web.

Purpose: to give information about _____

Audience: other students

Style: _____

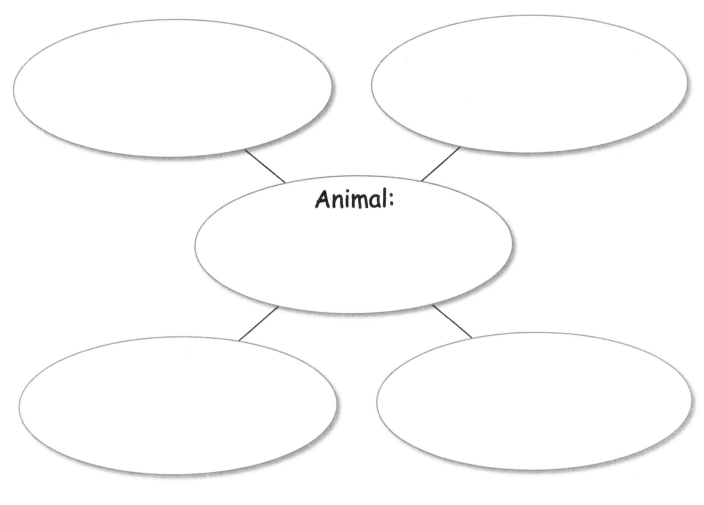

Animal:

 **Voice**

Use your web from Day 4 to write about an interesting animal.
Choose a writing style that is funny, serious, or exciting.

Be sure to use **a** and **an** correctly.

_____

_____

_____

_____

_____

_____

_____

_____

_____

_____

_____

_____

_____

 **Voice** A mood makes you feel a certain way.
Words and pictures create a mood.

A. Read each sentence. Look at the picture.
   Circle the word that tells the mood.

Justin is quietly sleeping in his bed.

angry   peaceful

The old, dirty bear was sitting alone in the corner.

sad   cheerful

B. Draw a picture with a happy mood.

C. Reread the sentences in Activity A. Which words end in **ing**?
   Write them on the lines.

_____   _____

 **Voice** Match the mood to your topic.

A. Think about a magical castle from long, long ago.
   Finish the sentences.

The Magical Castle

Example:

You won't see robots flying.

You will see a king and a queen feasting.

Word Box	
princess	knight
singing	laughing
unicorn	dragon

1. You won't see a farmer in a truck.

   You will see a _____.

2. You won't hear a school bell ringing.

   You will hear a _____ _____.

3. You won't pet a giraffe.

   You will pet a friendly _____.

B. Write a sentence about something that happens in the castle.

   _____

   _____

Daily 6-Trait Writing • EMC 6792 • © Evan-Moor Corp.

 **Voice**   Use adjectives and verbs to create a mood.

Read each cinquain. Underline the two adjectives.
Circle the three verbs ending in **ing**. Write the word
from the box that best describes the mood of the poem.

Word Box
angry
fun
exciting

Piggy Bank
Round, fat
Shaking, shaking, shaking
Nothing will come out!
Money-eater

Mood:

Treasure
Shiny, gold
Hiding, digging, finding
We'll follow the map
Loot

Mood:

Blueberry
Juicy, blue
Finding, picking, eating
Turns my teeth blue
Snack

Mood:

 **Voice**   Create a mood with a poem.

Use this chart to write a cinquain. Write about a food that is fun to eat. Create a fun mood!

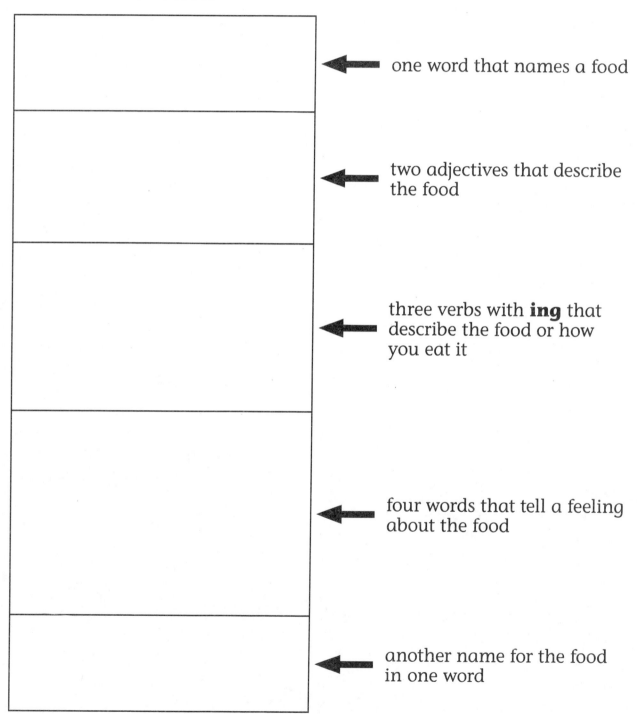

← one word that names a food

← two adjectives that describe the food

← three verbs with **ing** that describe the food or how you eat it

← four words that tell a feeling about the food

← another name for the food in one word

Daily 6-Trait Writing • EMC 6792 • © Evan-Moor Corp.

Voice

Copy the cinquain you wrote on Day 4 and draw a picture that adds to the mood. Then write a sentence that tells why your food is fun to eat.

Be sure words that end in **ing** are spelled correctly.

 **Voice** Every story has a point of view, or whose side the story is told from.

A. Read each sentence. Decide whose point of view it is.
   Circle the name.

"Feed me. I'm hungry!"

mother   baby

"Here's a tasty breakfast."

bird   snail

"I'm so glad to see you!"

cat   dog

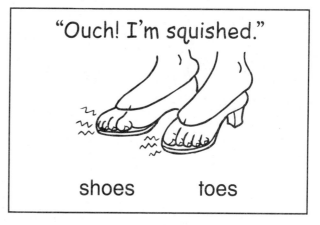

"Ouch! I'm squished."

shoes   toes

B. Whose point of view is it? Write an animal's name.

   "I'm staying in my shell! Make that cat go away,"

   said the _____.

C. An exclamation point (!) shows strong feeling.
   Circle the exclamation points on this page.

     Daily 6-Trait Writing • EMC 6792 • © Evan-Moor Corp.

 **Voice** A character's words and thoughts can tell you his or her point of view.

A. Look at the comic strip. Read each sentence. Decide whose point of view it is. Circle **grasshopper** or **elephant**.

The Grasshopper and the Elephant

He hopped on my toe!
grasshopper
elephant

Ow! That really hurt!
grasshopper
elephant

It's a nice day for a hop.
grasshopper
elephant

Oops! I didn't see him there.
grasshopper
elephant

B. What do you think the bird might be thinking?
Write a sentence that ends with an exclamation point.

_____

_____

 **Voice**   Write from a character's point of view.

A. Read the stories. Look and listen for the point of view.
    Circle the answer to each question.

Jack and the Beanstalk

Jack sold his mother's cow for magic beans. She threw them out, and a huge beanstalk grew! So Jack climbed to the top. There, he found a goose that laid golden eggs. It belonged to a giant. Jack took the goose and ran! The giant chased him down the beanstalk, but he couldn't catch Jack.

Who is telling the story?   Jack   a storyteller   a giant

My Golden Goose

I lived a happy life in my giant castle in the sky. I had all the gold I wanted. My beautiful goose laid golden eggs. Then one day a sneaky little boy climbed up a beanstalk. He came right into my home and stole my goose! I tried to catch him. But he scurried down the beanstalk. Then he chopped it down before I could follow him. I'll get him someday!

Who is telling the story?   a boy   the giant   a storyteller

B. Write two sentences to begin the story of "Jack and the Beanstalk."
    Write them from the point of view of the golden goose.

_____

_____

 **Voice**   Write from different points of view.

Look at the picture story. Think about what each character might be saying or thinking. Write from each character's point of view.

1

Wolf: _____

_____

_____

2

Little Pig: _____

_____

_____

3

Wolf: _____

_____

Little Pig: _____

_____

 **Voice**

Write an ending to "The Three Little Pigs." Write it from the point of view of the Wolf or one of the Pigs. Use your ideas from Day 4.

Use an exclamation point to show strong feeling.

_____

_____

_____

_____

_____

_____

_____

_____

_____

_____

_____

_____

_____

_____

Daily 6-Trait Writing • EMC 6792 • © Evan-Moor Corp.

 **Voice** Use formal and informal language.

A. Read each letter. Is the language formal or informal? Mark the answer with an **X**.

| Dear Mr. Evans,
Thank you for making puppets with us. I am not going to forget the fun we had.

_____ formal   _____ informal | Hi Emma!
It's me, Casey! Guess what! We made the coolest puppets out of old socks at school!

_____ formal   _____ informal |

B. What will you do this weekend? Write one sentence telling about it in formal language. Then write one sentence telling about it in informal language.

Formal: _____

_____

Informal: _____

_____

C. Write the words that would best replace the word **ain't** in these sentences.

1. Morgan ain't going with us.   _____

2. Talking penguins ain't her favorite.   _____

3. I ain't sure what time the movie starts.   _____

 **Voice** | Use different writing styles.

A. Read the story. Then answer the questions.

Pinocchio's Problem

Pinocchio is a wooden puppet with a good heart. But sometimes he is dishonest. One day, a man gives him 5 coins to give to his poor father. But Pinocchio keeps the money. When the Good Fairy asks him about the coins, he says that he lost them. But they are not lost. They are really in his pocket. Guess what happens! Because he isn't telling the truth, his nose grows two inches! Then he lies again and tells the Fairy he swallowed the coins. His nose grows even longer! It is so long that he begins bumping into walls. It takes him a long time to learn his lesson.

1. Did the writer use a funny or a serious writing style?

    _____

2. The writer wanted to teach a serious lesson in a fun way. Write the lesson of the story. Use a serious voice.

    _____

    _____

B. Cross out the word **ain't** in each sentence below. Write better words in its place. Check your work by looking in the story.

1. They ain't lost.   2. He ain't telling the truth.

 **Voice** Create a mood.

A. Read the story starter. Use proofreading marks to fix the use of **ain't**.

     Aaron and Cho had been hiking for many hours. Then it grew dark. They heard many strange noises.

     "Woooo! Woooo!"

     "That ain't an owl," whispered Aaron.

     "I think we should go home now. This ain't fun anymore," Cho said.

     "You're right," said Aaron, looking around. "But where is home?"

B. Finish the story. Create a spooky mood.

_____

_____

_____

_____

_____

_____

Voice   Write from different points of view.

Think about the story of "Little Red Riding Hood."
Write what each person would say.

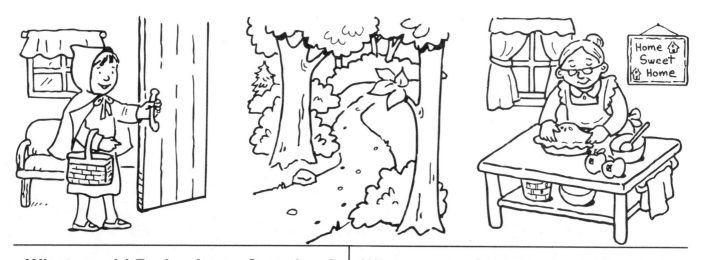

What would Red write to Grandma?	**What would Grandma write to Red?**

Daily 6-Trait Writing • EMC 6792 • © Evan-Moor Corp.

 **Voice**

Write a letter from the point of view of Red Riding Hood or Grandmother. Use your chart from Day 4.

Use **isn't**, **aren't**, or **am not** instead of **ain't**.

_____

_____

_____

_____

_____

_____

_____

_____

_____

_____

_____

_____

_____

Proofreading Marks

Mark	Meaning	Example
ℐ	Take this out (delete).	I love ~~to~~ to read.
⊙	Add a period.	It was late⊙
☰	Make this a capital letter.	First prize went to <u>maria</u>.
/	Make this a lowercase letter.	We saw a Black Cat.
———	Fix the spelling.	This is our ~~hause~~ house.
⋏	Add a comma.	Goodnight⋏ Mom.
⋁	Add an apostrophe.	That⋁s Lil⋁s bike.
! ? ∧ ∧	Add an exclamation point or a question mark.	Help∧! Can you help me∧?
∧	Add a word or a letter.	The∧ red pen is mine.
# ∧	Add a space between words.	I like∧# pizza.
———	Underline the words.	We read <u>Old Yeller</u>.

Daily 6-Trait Writing • EMC 6792 • © Evan-Moor Corp.